THE
ORPHAN
TRAINS

A HISTORY PERSPECTIVES BOOK

Peggy Caravantes

Massanutten Regional Library
174 South Main Street
Harrisonburg, VA 22801

J 362.73 C

Published in the United States of America by Cherry Lake Publishing
Ann Arbor, Michigan
www.cherrylakepublishing.com

Consultants: Jason LaBau, PhD, U.S. History, Lecturer, California State
Polytechnic University, Pomona; Marla Conn, ReadAbility, Inc.
Editorial direction: Red Line Editorial
Book design and illustration: Sleeping Bear Press

Photo Credits: North Wind Picture Archives/AP Images, cover (left), 1
(left); Kansas State Historical Society, cover (middle), 1 (middle), 8;
National Orphan Train Complex, cover (right), 1 (right), 4, 10, 15, 18, 24,
27, 30; North Wind/North Wind Picture Archives, 5, 21; Library of
Congress, 12, 17, 20, 22

Copyright ©2014 by Cherry Lake Publishing
All rights reserved. No part of this book may be reproduced or utilized in
any form or by any means without written permission from the publisher.

Library of Congress Cataloging-in-Publication Data
Caravantes, Peggy, 1935-
  The orphan trains / Peggy Caravantes.
    pages cm – (Perspectives library)
  ISBN 978-1-62431-420-9 (hardcover) – ISBN 978-1-62431-496-4 (pbk.)
– ISBN 978-1-62431-458-2 (pdf) – ISBN 978-1-62431-534-3 (ebook)
 1. Orphan trains–History–Juvenile literature. 2. Orphans–United States–
History–Juvenile literature. I. Title.
HV985.C37 2014
362.734–dc23

                                   2013006360

Cherry Lake Publishing would like to acknowledge the work of
The Partnership for 21st Century Skills. Please visit *www.p21.org*
for more information.

Printed in the United States of America
Corporate Graphics Inc.
July 2013
CLFA11

TABLE OF CONTENTS

In this book, you will read about the orphan trains from three perspectives. From 1854 to 1929, orphan trains brought orphans and poor children from the crowded East Coast to better homes in the Midwest and West. Each perspective is based on real things that happened to real people who experienced the orphan trains. As you'll see, the same event can look different depending on one's point of view.

1

James Sinclair

Orphan

After Mama died from **tuberculosis** in 1909, Papa tried to take care of me. But he got hurt while working on the docks in New York City later that year. Soon after, he lost his job and didn't have any money to buy food or pay rent on our room. Papa took me to a Children's Aid Society **orphanage** in 1910. He told me he would come back to get me when he got well and had a job again. I hated going there—I wasn't an orphan. I had Papa. He made me go though.

The day Papa took me to the orphanage, I was scared. It was a huge, redbrick building with so many windows. I was afraid I would get lost in there. I hung on to Papa's hand and begged him not to leave me. But he said he couldn't take care of me right now.

I tried to be brave at the orphanage. I knew that many children had to live on the streets. At least at the orphanage I had someone to take care of me. After I had been there about six months, a man named Mr. Adams talked to some of us

A goal of the orphan trains was to get children out of crowded orphanages and place them with families who could raise them. ▶

boys. He said he had good news for us. We were going on a train trip to a better place. In Kansas, each of us would live with an adult couple who would take care of us.

I told Mr. Adams I didn't want to go. Papa wouldn't know where I was when he came to get me. Mr. Adams pulled me aside and put his arm around

SEVENTY-FIVE YEARS

During a 75-year period, orphan trains carried about 120,000 children from New York to new homes. The orphan trains were a program of the Children's Aid Society. The trains traveled to more than 45 states, although most of them went to the Midwest and the West. Changes in society gradually resulted in more children being placed locally. The last train traveled to Texas in 1929.

my shoulders. He told me Papa had died from the injuries he suffered when he got hurt at the docks. I really was an orphan.

That night we took baths and got haircuts. Early the next morning, Miss Lane brought me new clothes: **knickers**, a suit coat, a dress shirt, a tie, and a pair of shiny, black boots. Miss Lane helped take care of the kids at the orphanage. She said she would be going on the train with us. Miss Lane gave me a small **satchel**. Inside were a change of clothes and a Bible. I had nothing else to put in it.

The next morning we went to the train station. On the first day and night, we traveled from New York to Chicago, Illinois. We slept in our seats. At Union Station the next morning, we got on another train that was headed to Kansas. I was told it was in the Midwest.

During the ride I saw things I had never seen before—cornfields, red apple orchards, piles of yellow pumpkins, and lots of cows. Not all of the trip was

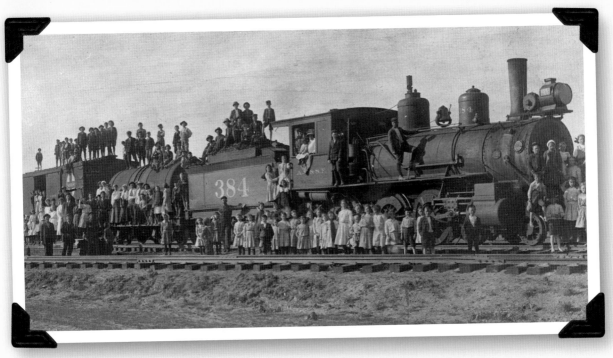

▲ *Large groups of kids could be brought west at once.*

good. I got tired of having milk and red jelly
sandwiches three times a day.

I was glad when we finally got to Coffeyville,
Kansas, but then I saw the big crowd of people
waiting at the station. They stared at us as we walked
across the street to a church. Inside a big room, there
were ten chairs lined up on a stage. Miss Lane told
us to take a chair and sit up straight.

The crowd followed us in. A man got up and talked to the people. Then Miss Lane stepped to the front of the stage. One by one she called us to stand beside her so she could introduce us. When it was my turn, she said my name was James Sinclair and that I was ten years old.

After we had all gone on stage, the people came closer and stared at us some more. One man squeezed my arm and walked away. Most just looked at me from my feet to my head. Another man stuck his finger in my mouth to check my teeth. I didn't like that. His finger tasted like dirt.

Most of the strangers went back to their seats. I started to worry. What if the man who poked my teeth picked me? What if no one chose me and I had to get back on the train?

SECOND SOURCE

▶ Find another source that tells the story about how the orphan train children were presented to townspeople. Compare the information in that source to what you read here.

9

▲ *Orphans were lined up so potential parents could look at them.*

Then a gray-haired couple motioned for me to come to them. I looked at Miss Lane and she nodded. I wasn't sure. When the couple smiled, though, I walked from the stage and joined them. They introduced themselves as Mr. and Mrs. King. They said they never had a child of their own. They wanted me to come live with them. The lady was nice, and she told me to call her Mama King. She took one of my hands. Mr. King grabbed my satchel and my other hand. We walked out of the church. Another couple walked by and asked Mr. King who I was. He put his arm around my shoulder and said, "This is my son, James."

THINK ABOUT IT

▶ Determine the main point of this paragraph and pick out one piece of evidence that supports it.

2

Nancy King
Midwestern Farmer

It was in March 1910 that I first noticed the poster at the general store. It announced that families were needed to care for orphan children from New York. The children would be presented at the Methodist church as soon as the train arrived. I told my husband, George, about the poster. I asked him what he thought about us taking in an orphan. We have no children of our own. Now that we are getting older, it would be nice to have a young one around—to add some spirit to our old farmhouse.

He frowned and shook his head. Then he reminded me of what happened to his cousin Samuel, who took in a boy named Peter last year. The first afternoon Peter was there, Samuel took him all around the farm. The boy especially liked the baby chicks that were in cages with their mothers. Samuel said they would let the chicks out the next morning.

What happened next was just terrible for a farmer. Before breakfast, Peter slipped out and went to the chicken cages. He opened all the doors, releasing the baby chicks. After breakfast, Samuel took the boy with him while he made his rounds. Peter could

SECOND SOURCE

▶ Find another source that describes how towns announced the opportunity to get a child from an orphan train. Compare the information in that source to what you read here.

hardly wait for them to get to the cages. But when they got there, Samuel and Peter stared in horror at the dead chicks on the cold, wet grass. Peter hadn't known they could not be released until the sun had dried the dew. I think Peter wanted Samuel to like him so much that he got up early to surprise his new father. Maybe he thought Samuel would like his early morning help. Even with Peter's good intentions, Samuel decided he didn't need that kind of help. He sent Peter back.

I told my husband that wasn't likely to happen again. We didn't even have any baby chicks. He just shook his head. Then on Sunday morning in church, the preacher talked about the orphan train that was going to come. He again invited people to take one of the children into their homes.

ANALYZE THIS

▶ Find another perspective that discusses how orphans could be sent back. How are the two perspectives alike? How are they different?

The family must take care of the child's needs— food, clothing, education, and religious instruction. In return, the child could provide extra labor on the farm. Anyone interested must make an appointment to be interviewed by the town committee, the group that decided who should receive a child.

▲ *Some orphans who were placed with families were sent back to New York because the placement did not work.*

FIRST ORPHAN TRAIN

The first orphan train went to Dowagiac, Michigan, in 1854. Log cabin homes, a tavern, a post office, a railroad station, and one church made up the town. The group included more than 30 boys from six to 15 years old. Nine of the youngest boys were not chosen and had to board the train to seek a home elsewhere.

My husband and I talked about it some more on the way home after church. George didn't seem quite so opposed this time. While I got Sunday dinner on the table, he went off for a walk. When he came back, he said that he had thought about it, and we could take a child. I was thrilled and glad George would have a helper. We made an appointment for an interview. After they asked questions about my husband's job, what property we owned, and our church attendance, we were approved. On Friday morning, we waited at the station with the rest of the big crowd for the orphan train to arrive.

Ten boys got off the train. Their clothes were wrinkled, and their hair was going every which way. They looked at the ground as they were led to the church auditorium. Inside, the **placing agent**, who had come with the boys on the train, introduced them. One boy caught our attention from the moment we saw him on the stage. He sat stiffly with his fists clenched. I could tell he was scared but trying not to show it. When he was introduced, we learned his name was James Sinclair and that he was ten years old.

Interviews for potential parents often took place in churches. ▼

▲ *Once chosen, boys and girls often helped out at their new parents' homes and farms.*

When the introductions were over, everyone rushed to the stage to get a better look at the boys. We held back for a few minutes and watched James. He tried to smile when people spoke to him. I saw him flinch when Old Man Gunther stuck his finger in the boy's mouth, checking his teeth, I suppose. He ought to know better—these were children, not horses!

George and I walked up to the stage and motioned for James to come down on the floor with us. He hesitated and looked at Miss Lane, who nodded. We smiled at him, and he came to meet us. I introduced my husband and myself. I took his hand and told him to call me Mama King. Then George grabbed the boy's satchel and his other hand.

Just as we got outside, some friends walked up. They asked who we had with us. George looked down at the boy, put his arm around his shoulders, and said, "This is my son, James." I could tell my husband was proud to have a new son.

3

Anna Lane

Placing Agent

I became a **social worker** for the Children's Aid Society in 1900 and have worked with the organization for ten years. Although I had a teaching **certificate**, I decided to become a social worker when I saw all the children, from toddlers to teens, who lived on the streets of New York City. During the day, they wandered around and searched

▲ *During the time of the orphan trains, many homeless children roamed and slept on the streets of New York City.*

through garbage cans for food. At night they slept in doorways, on piles of trash, or in cardboard boxes.

I was hired to work in one of the orphanages of the Children's Aid Society. The children here are the lucky ones, I guess. They have a bed, food, and clothes.

▲ *Charles Loring Brace began the orphan trains to help children without parents find new families.*

Only about half of them are orphans. Many of the kids—about 25 percent—have both parents still living. But for different reasons, the parents can't or won't take care of them.

In 1854, Charles Loring Brace began what came to be called the "orphan train" program. There were so many children in the orphanage that Mr. Brace decided to send as many as possible to other states. Mr. Brace felt that institutions were not the best environment for children. He believed they needed

CHARLES LORING BRACE

Charles Loring Brace founded the Children's Aid Society in 1853. Brace, who was a minister, believed all children needed good homes, education, and jobs. He used the Society to send orphans and children whose parents couldn't take care of them by train from the slums of New York City to farms in the Midwest. There, local residents could select a child and had the choice to become **foster parents** or adopt the child.

good homes where they would be taught about the Bible and learn a trade. Because farmers in so many states never had enough labor, he decided sending children to midwestern states would benefit both them and farmers. By the time I was approached about becoming a placing agent for ten boys being

▲ *Brace thought orphans could help out on farms in the Midwest.*

sent to Coffeyville, Kansas, the Children's Aid Society had already sent thousands of children by train to new homes.

That did not mean the process always went smoothly. Some people felt the orphan trains were a way to dump unwanted children from the East Coast in other cities. States had begun to pass laws making the process illegal. Even where it was still acceptable, the placement process could be difficult. There was an incident in an Arizona town where people fought over the orphans. The night after their placement, many orphans were given to new families because some people believed the first families did not fit well with the kids. Other orphans were forced to leave town and return to New York.

I knew that previous groups of children sent to be placed were sometimes as large as 100. I felt fortunate that I was taking only ten boys. Still, I felt nervous. Would I be able to manage them? What would happen if I couldn't find homes for all of them? The night before we left, I helped see that the boys had baths and got haircuts. I laid out a new set of clothes and a pair of shoes for each boy. I put a change of clothes and a Bible into each of their satchels.

The next morning we made our way to the train station. I was able to keep up with the boys and not lose them in the crowd. Once we were on the train and settled into our seats, I relaxed a little. Most of the boys had never been outside New York, and all the sights fascinated them. I answered many questions as the train rolled west.

On Friday, we reached Coffeyville, Kansas. A large crowd of curious townspeople and potential parents waited for us at the **depot** of the small farming community. I led the

ANALYZE THIS

▶ Find another chapter that discusses orphans first meeting townspeople. How are the viewpoints alike? How are they different?

▲ *For the most part, orphans were excited to be chosen by families.*

boys off the train and across the street to a church. The crowd followed us. The church's pastor spoke to them for a few minutes. He reminded them that only those already approved by the town's committee could take a child. Then he asked me to introduce the boys.

After I introduced all the boys, the crowd drew to the stage to get a closer look. A few couples immediately selected a child. Others looked them over and walked away. James Sinclair stood alone until a gray-haired couple motioned for him to come off the stage and talk to them. He hesitated and looked at me. When I nodded my approval, he joined them. After they had talked for a few minutes, I went over and whispered in James's ear that I would come back next year to check on him and that he could write to me. We wanted to make sure that his new family treated him well. He smiled bravely, and I walked away to help some of the other boys.

When I looked again, James was leaving the church, holding hands with the older couple. I prayed that he and all the other boys would be happy in their new homes. I was so grateful that all ten had been chosen. I had been a little worried about James and some of the other younger boys. Experienced placing agents had told me that the youngest ones were sometimes not chosen. People did not believe they would be good workers. I was thankful to be able to get back on a train without needing to take any of the boys to another town. As I left, I saw James's new father put his arm around him, and I knew that he would have a happy home.

THINK ABOUT IT

▶ Determine the main idea of this paragraph. Pick out one piece of evidence that supports the main idea.

Massanutten Regional Library
174 South Main Street
Harrisonburg, VA 22801

LOOK, LOOK AGAIN

This photograph shows a group of orphans who have just arrived in a town and will soon be displayed to the townspeople. Use the photograph to answer the following questions:

1. Imagine you are one of these orphans. What would be your biggest worry? What could you do to stand out from the others so a family would select you?

2. Imagine you are hoping to be a foster parent. How would you describe this scene in a letter to your family?

3. Imagine you are a social worker. What would you do to help these orphans in your care be chosen by a family?

GLOSSARY

certificate (sur-TIF-uh-kit) a piece of paper that officially states something is so, such as a person being qualified to practice teaching

depot (DEE-poh) a railroad station

foster parent (FAWS-tur PAIR-uhnt) an adult who raises a child who is not his or her own, without adopting the child

knickers (NIH-kurs) loose trousers with short legs that are gathered in a band just below the knee

orphanage (OR-fuh-nij) a public building where orphans live and are cared for

placing agent (PLAE-sing AY-juhnt) a social worker assigned to find homes for children on the orphan trains

satchel (SAH-chuhl) a small suitcase

social worker (SOH-shuhl WUR-kur) a person whose job is to provide services, such as food, housing, education, and health care, to those who cannot help themselves

tuberculosis (tu-bur-kyuh-LOH-sis) a contagious disease caused by bacteria that affects the lungs and bones

LEARN MORE

Further Reading

Kay, Verla. *Orphan Train*. New York: G. P. Putnam's Sons, 2003.

Littlefield, Holly. *Children of the Orphan Trains*. Minneapolis, MN: Carolrhoda Books, 2001.

Warren, Andrea. *We Rode the Orphan Trains*. Boston: Houghton Mifflin, 2004.

Web Sites

National Orphan Train Complex
http://orphantraindepot.org
This Web site has stories of orphans who rode the orphan trains.

The Orphan Trains
http://www.childrensaidsociety.org/about/history/orphan-trains
At this Web site, readers can learn more about the history of the orphan trains.

INDEX

ABOUT THE AUTHOR

Peggy Caravantes is the author of middle-grade and young-adult biographies as well as nonfiction books for elementary students. She lives in San Antonio, Texas.